RAISED IN THE SHADOW

*A Collection of Twenty-five Poems
by
Phillip Rosenberg*

To Gus Hadorn, who sent out the call

Special Thanks to Catherine Svehla for the momentum

Copyright © 1997 by Phillip Rosenberg
3rd Printing, 2007

ISBN 978-0-9659965-5-6
ISBN-10 0-9659965-5-7

All rights reserved. No part of any of this book may be reproduced in any form or by any electronic or mechanical means including information storage and retrieval systems without permission in writing from the publisher, except by a reviewer who may quote passages in a review.

Artwork by Elyse Adler

Cover and Page Layout by Bart Dawson

"My Father's World" and "Loving with Effort" previously published in Black Moon.

RAISED
IN THE
SHADOW

*A Collection of Twenty-five Poems
by
Phillip Rosenberg*

1997
SUNLAND PRESS
NASHVILLE, TENNESSEE

*Eva —
Thanks for connecting!
— Dallis (RAGS)*

> "I was raised in the shadow,
> but I'm walking toward the light..."
>
> — Tom Kimmel and Amy Powers

Contents

Foreword   9

I

Ambition	12
A Mother's Love	14
I-40	15
To Francis	16
My Father's World	18
Vacuum	20
Your Place	23
Possum	27

II

A Corner Turned	30
Wanting	34
This Is Not My Life	35
The Archers	36
A Change of Quality	37
It's Always Something	38
Loving With Effort	39
Today	41

III

In the Present, Suddenly	44
Skydreamer	46
Where I Am Going	47
I Want To Lie Here	50
Advice To A Father	52
In Your Grief	53
The Moon	54
To Jessie	56
The Way I Love You	58

Foreword to the 10th Anniversary Edition

This collection was written as my farewell to a faithfully attempted songwriting career in Nashville, Tennessee. I was a single father, struggling financially, and unconvinced I had anything worth saying. I was approaching fifty.

I was introduced to several poets and a handful of poems that spoke so directly to my personal experience that it startled me: Mary Oliver, David Whyte, Ranier Maria Rilke, William Butler Yeats, Robert Francis. Here was a new language, one with a vocabulary that seemed capable of expressing what seemed like the otherwise inexplicable truth of my experience.

The first two printings of *Raised In The Shadow* sold out, but by then I was busy as a building contractor and a father. After a time, I forgot I ever published a book of poetry. Several years ago, I received a call from a woman who purchased a copy of this book in a used bookstore and wanted another. She tracked me down. No, I was sorry to report, I had no copies to sell. I did not even own a copy myself. Even today, as I tell you this, I am astonished at how completely I abandoned my creative life.

Thank you for joining me on the pages of this modest collection of poems and for your willingness to imagine something useful might be found here.

Phillip Rosenberg
Spring, 2007

I

Ambition

You knew of a place
he did not know;
perhaps you'd seen it in magazines or
heard tell of it from friends;
but he was content right where he was
with canned vegetables
and Gunsmoke;
you heard arias in your head
but he could not hear you,
and you could not see
how to remain there with him in
that simple-ness
as night after night
that train roared through your dreams
undeniably headed
toward the other side of town.

The day came
when you sat us down, my sister and I,
opened our chests
with a few careful, sharp words and
removed half our hearts;
Now, all these years later,

I still sit at my desk
scratching paper with #2 pencil
as if I could
stop this itch,
as if I could be complete,
as if this phantom pain
would go away.

A Mother's Love

It was an act of love:
my mother beating me like that
until I lay crumpled
on the wet green tile
in my tears and
the hard spray of the shower;

At barely 9 years old,
with water snaking out of the
tarnished chrome nozzle
I had suddenly discovered
my nakedness and at once asked
my father to leave the room;

It is a twist of fate
a son wounding the father
and though he walked away
his silent grief tore at his face
so mother in her love for him
raged for once when he could not.

I-40

Once, as a young boy, driving home with dad in his
old green work van, he sighed: "You know, son,
sometimes I feel like I want to just keep on driving."
It was many years before I understood his meaning:
how job and family can imprison a man
behind the bars of someone else's expectations.

A few hard highway miles of my own behind me, I
found myself mouthing exactly his words to my 10-year
old son. In that moment, it felt like the ends of a circle
were joined, a circle with an ancient circumference
on which each of us finds his place. For me, it happened
in a '77 Silverado on a long stretch of I-40
headed west into the sun.

To Francis

You lived
in her house
long after most daughters
have left to make lives of their own;
but you could not
make it on your own.
You could not
take care of yourself.
You were sick.
You needed her.
You believed that
and from that
she spun the web
that held you
all those dark years.

The time came
when your rage saved you;
you pulled that dagger
from your breast
and severed every tie
cleanly
finally.

You and I haven't spoken in years

I tell people you are estranged
from the family.
When asked, you tell people
you have no family;
they are dead,
and I suppose we are.

Mother called me last night.
At the end of our conversation
she wondered aloud
where you were.
She said:
"I just want to know she's all right."

And in our old mother's sweet voice
I heard a rumbling
deep and terrifying
and all I could think of
was to call out to you
wherever you are:
Run! Run as fast as you can and
don't look back.

My Father's World

They came in white laboratory coats
soldering under microscopes
in dust-free rooms,
pushing my father's world of blunt tools aside.
That world is fading slowly now into
the cracks of an old man's memory.
It can barely be seen
through the dark glass. Look!
Do you see that ball-peen hammer?
The chisels laid out
evenly on the wooden bench?
They appear Neolithic;
relics of another way of
moving mountains.

My father lives marginally
in this modern world.
After eighty-three years
he's taken to preaching.
Eight or ten people gather
in someone's living room
and listen to his account of dying
on the operating table.
They support him with love offerings.
Occasionally, he loses his place and

thinks he's back in the shipyard
doing an important job;
the men in laboratory coats
remove him quickly and ask
him to not return.

Vacuum

I think it was 1977
when she first
started drinking.
Over the years
her once clear mind
became soft and dull;
her talk became babbled.
But I didn't see it
until it was too late,
until she'd been completely
gutted.
Why?

It is commonly known
the human brain
inherently inverts
left and right
and is itself divided
functionally
down the middle.

Lesser know
but of far wider
implication
is the other great
cerebral inversion:

that of positive and negative space.

When I looked
at that person
I loved,
my brain
told me she was still there
within that border of flesh.

The reality
as I now know it
is that she left long ago;
the outline I saw
was created where
the familiar background
of furniture, appliances
and children
met nothingness.

This was my brain's
clever and kind way
of handling no-thing-ness.
Think of it as the emotional analogy to
"nature abhors a vacuum".
My brain simply rushed in to fill that negative space
with hair, a simile,

an old blue flannel shirt.
But when I tried to touch her,
my hand passed
right through
to the stained walls.

Your Place

It is Sunday;
I wake up on your sofa,
A curtain of rain
dripping opaquely from the eave
down the windowpane,
a black and white reflection
appears
to float in the
leaf-collage beyond
the glass;
the sound is disconnected from the visual
and comes from behind and above me,
splashing insistently through
the downspouts;
I feel like an intruder here
in your world;
the wind comes,
pushes the branches
around silently,
unseen,
like me;
the wind's presence is felt,
passes on,
affects,
but remains unaffected;
rootless,

but with the power
to uproot;
transient,
wild,
homeless;
I have always been
drawn to the wind;
standing,
eyes closed,
facing into the mystery,
feeling it
gently caress my cheek
like a lover;

I get up and make
coffee;
tiptoe,
try not to wake you from
your sleepy solitude in
the other end of your home;

Women marry,
move into a man's home,
make it their own,
somehow;

I cannot find

the way to do that here;

I discuss it with the wind
who understands
my position
completely
and sympathizes.

"If you long for permanence"
says the wind,
"Go to the mountains and
talk to the rocks.
They know all about that".

Why bother
I think,
the rocks don't know me;
But suddenly I remember
fifteen;
climbing the San Gabriel Mountains
as close to death
as I've ever been
on that sheer face with Eddie Kohn,
moving slowly,
hand hold to hand hold
clinging to that rock

in spite of gravity;
the stone spoke to me then;
it said:
"Move slowly,
be deliberate,
have patience",
and I did.

The rain has stopped,
the eave is still
dripping lightly,
the leaves are motionless;
the bobwhites,
cardinals and mocking birds discuss
the changing weather;
my coffiee is ready;
you will sleep
another hour and
dream another song.

Maybe I'll get dressed
and take a walk,
or pick a book from your shelf
at random,
turn to the middle
and begin reading
as if I belonged there.

Possum

As if it weren't bad enough
that the lifeless body of the possum
lay in the middle of the road for three days,
Friday night it was forced to suffer
the ignominy of being
flattened by a pickup truck full of
middle-class teenagers.

Saturday morning,
as I drove past,
what was left of the broken face
stared back and spoke to me,
saying: "This is good balancing out evil;
this is justice being done;
this is the kind universe
manifesting itself.
This is a man who never smoked
dying of lung cancer."

RNER TURNED

I painted one wall in my bedroom
Chinese red,
hung black carpet on another,
poked holes in a cardboard box
filled with flashing Christmas lights
to shine stars on the ceiling
and lived there in that
teenage womb
until I was ready to be born
at seventeen.
Mom stood on the porch
saying: "If you leave now
don't ever come back."
But birth is supposed to be painful,
and so I passed
irrevocably
down through that angry
threatening uterus
of Foothill Boulevard
and out into the wonderfully mad
world of college girls,
marijuana,
homosexuals,
revolutionaries,
rock 'n rollers,

vegetarians,
intellectuals,
rednecks and there I was
with no one to say
"This way!" or
"Be careful there."
Only an occasional call
from dad, usually when I was stoned,
asking if I would reconsider
this musician stuff
and become a lawyer or a doctor.
And so I wandered,
pretty much aimlessly,
gathering the experience
one needs to gather
if they haven't
a lick of sense to
begin with and I guess
I did that for about thirty years.

So here I am today,
a buddhist-jew-boy
carpenter in the south,
living from job to job
and sometimes I think
my whole life was
one long detour;

as if someday I'll
get back to that main road,
the one all the normal kids took
when they got out of high school.
But I know better;
They all took their own roads.
Some were more fucked up
than mine
and the beaver cleaver
homes I imagined they all had
were full of the same
sort of silent paint I felt
in the abyss
of my aloneness.
At least in my case
a healing of sorts has begun
and now I know where
I am and
somewhere along the way
children happened and to them
I can say: "This way" and
"Be careful over there"
and sometimes a feeling of
blessedness comes
like Wordsworth had on that
two mile walk
and extraordinary people
have come into my life

and if there is a main road,
it's the one we each blaze,
first with our grief
and then with our
faith and this one
is moving now after all these years
through Dante's dark woods
into the clearing
I always knew
existed and it's just like
being back in my
black and red bedroom
except with all my friends
and all of us with this
deep abiding feeling
of gratitude.

WANTING

You can want something
so much,
so long,
so badly,
when it finally comes
to your door
you mistake it for a beggar
and send it away;

The wanting
has become the end
in and of itself,
a mask,
rendering unrecognizable
the true nature of your desire;

Throw off your wanting
and you will see clearly
these gifts
that come to visit you;

Admit them all!
Lavish them with
gratitude!

This Is Not My Life

This is not my life;
I do not live here, inside
this narrow arc of the sun;
here, where the distance
between events
is measured on
someone else's clock!
This is not my life
passing from day to day
buried under a pile of work
on someone else's list of
important things.

No, my life is over there;

Look carefully:
You can see me
walking now,
steady and calm,
catching up with my own
footsteps.

The Archers

They are moving quietly
through the shadows,
barely below the threshold of
my discomfort;
They are whispering:
Calling out my true name,
the one I forgot;
They are tugging,
insistent, forceful,
their firm dark hands
on the blades
of my shoulder,
turning me first this way,
then that;
Like an arrow,
they aim me
with tender merciless love,
directly toward the center of my fear,
their exquisite accuracy measured
unerringly by the windsock of my resistance.

It is an oddly practical dynamic:
the harder I struggle,
the clearer their target.

A Change of Quality

The dew gathers at the tip
of the leaf,
swells,
slow and imperceptible,
like a shadow
moves across
the face of
a sundial until

suddenly:
the weight of the droplet
overcomes
it's own surface tension;

the tiny tear drops away,
the leaf lifts and
shudders lightly.

In that decisive moment
everything changes.

ALWAYS SOMETHING

It's always something, isn't it?
Always something
not quite finished,
not quite right,
needs a nudge this way or that.
But what else would you expect?
What does it mean,
"A body at rest?"
Nothing is ever truly complete
except in death,
and that only a process
concealed from our view.

Reaching for the unattainable
may be our most human quality,
and what most endears us to the gods;
in the end,
it's our longing for perfection,
our secret desire
to break ourselves
against the unbreakable,
that drives us finally
into the naked, graceful embrace
of our own sweet imperfect nature.

Loving With Effort

From deep in the distance
your voice shoots through the wire
leaving a wake of
sparks
a mile long;
taking out a transformer in
Tulsa,
Downing a pole in Dubuque,
arriving here
your words
rapid fire
find their mark
and I fall like a rootless hickory

When I love you
our words dance;
now, I stumble,
hesitate

consider,
think…

Loving with effort
is like trying to explain
a poem
and I've never been
very good at that.

Today

I'm not going to wash dishes today;
I'm not going to sweep or dust
or pick up after the children;
today, I am going to attend to other matters,
matters far more dusty and neglected.

I'm not going to run errands;
I'm not going to pay bills, go to the bank
or balance the checkbook;
today, I am going to attend to other matters,
matters far more out of balance.

I am not going to answer the phone today,
turn on the TV, or listen to the radio;
today, I am going to listen to smaller sounds,
those that call softly from beneath the
murky dark surface of this daily drudgery.

Today I am going to do the other work,
the truly important work;
today I will stand
against those forces that conspire
to condemn me to routine
and I will not yield;
this time,
they will have to
wait until tomorrow.

THE PRESENT, SUDDENLY

Your head is cradled in
the crook of my arm,
your deep, slow breathing soft
against the drip of the rain.
Outside, the sound of a car
on the wet pavement
propels me
into the moment:
A white doorframe stands suddenly
against the ochre wall;
Sounds are detached,
smaller;
You stretch across the pillow,
your back arched cat-like;
I want only to remain here,
moving in cognizance
through this eternal moment;
But I know the truth of it all too well:
Soon, I will be swept back into the rapids of the clock;
This landscape of simple pleasure,
this delight of detail
will again rush by,
blurred and peripheral;
Yet, this morning,

this moment,
now,
I am here;
You are here;
and God is everywhere;
in the lampshade
and in the worn, brown carpet.

Skydreamer

I was sleeping the deep sleep
of the sky dreamer
when I thought I heard someone
knocking;
Rising from my place
I opened the door only a crack;
there you stood,
covered in moon,
sparkled in star.
"Wake up, old man!" you said,
your smile broadening to the
horizons;
"But isn't it the middle of the night?"
"Yes! What better time to catch the sky dreams?"
I threw on my courage and,
checking my pockets, yelled in a panic:
"I can't find my net!"
"Oh, you silly man…" you purred,
 and gently pulled it from
behind my ear
just like my Uncle Manny
used to do with a quarter;
And you laughed:
"It was right there all the time!"

Where I Am Going

Once again,
clutter has claimed victory.
The days have become unmanageable;
Small pieces of life are breaking off and
slipping through the cracks,
lost forever;
Appointments are forgotten and
keys misplaced;
My firm resolve to aspire to the simple
echoes now like a distant cannon
firing the first shot of a battle already lost.
The hopeful young soldiers of organization
armed with the best of intention
were not overwhelmed quickly,
but overcome instead by attrition.
They were not defeated in a frontal assault,
but rather by a creeping
accumulation of camouflaged detail
noticed too late:
too many dishes in the sink,
no time to make the bed,
too many impossible places to be,
too far to travel
in too little time
and, finally, a checking account
beyond reconciliation.

I know the simple life I long for
is within my grasp;
It lies dead ahead,
just beyond this complexity of habit,
just over this hill of accumulation;
When I have the strength
I will regroup,
consolidate, eliminate, re-think.
I will have a garage sale;
I will sacrifice everything but
a small Oriental rug on the
polished maple floor,
a small oak writing desk
by the east window,
A vase on the mantle with flowers
cut fresh daily
from my small but spirited garden;
I will make the hard choices;
I will undress piece by piece
until I am naked,
until there is nothing left
for the enemy to take.

I will count the hours on
small Tibetan bells,
keep a cupboard with tea and rice;
I will keep fresh fruit on the
breakfast table,

and watch the morning light wash through
my house unobstructed.
I will walk a simple path,
unadorned except by
life's own sweet grace.

I Want To Lie Here

I want to lie here
next to you
in this naked stillness,
eye to eye,
no expectations,
no anticipation,
close, but
not touching,
until the space between us
trembles,
until I feel my heart
begin to rise
and flow
through the tips
of my fingers
onto the the surface
of your skin;

I want to lie here
next to you,
quietly
watching
your river
rise

like the Mississippi
until even the highest
banks
can not contain it,
until all the dams
collapse,
until it overflows into
every county
from Memphis to the Gulf;

I want to lie here
next to you
joined in this way
laughing wildly
until I drown in your passion,
until rescue is impossible,
until I wash ashore
all the while holding
your eyes in mine.

Advice To A Father

When you raise your voice
you're going in the
wrong direction;
Volume and power
are related
inversely;
go down, instead;
slip beneath the surface;
the deeper you go,
the quieter it becomes,
the easier to hear and
to be heard;

Be like the lion:
he settles the issue
with a yawn.

In Your Grief

On ordinary days
you keep yourself
behind a seductive smile;
Now, your tears wash that
façade away and
a deeper beauty is revealed
by the honesty of your loss;
Now, I see you clearly
against the sudden
dark shroud;
Grief becomes you.

The Moon

She is a lamp;
Her light is turned on
deliberately
and shaded just so
in a calculated effort to attract
and in this way,
night after night,
she relies on the moth's
longing for incandescence
to prove
her own irresistibility;

But you,
You are the moon,
naked and true
with nothing to prove;
the sun has chosen you
and you alone to
reflect his brilliance;
What then do you need with moths?
Wolves and coyotes
call to you,
lovers beg your favor,
poets invoke your name,

The seas rise and fall
at your command and I,
on this journey through the night,
would surely lose my way
if it were not for your gentle light
illuminating my path.

TO JESSIE

I found a butterfly wing
on the stone steps;
deep copper,
magic iridescence,
tiny yellow suns,
a microcosm of nature's perfect
attention to detail;
I carried it to the truck,
carefully placed
that delicacy
on the dirty rough seat;
It would be a gift
for my young daughter
still in her magic,
still child enough
to see
the magic in it;

I returned to work,
filled my head with measurements,
plans,
regrets,
imagined conversations,
the stuff work days

are made of;

It was the next day,
biking at the lake,
coming around a rocky bend,
I remembered the wing;
Of course, it could
not have survived;

Before long the
grit of life
will mercifully toughen her skin;
her wonder will retreat
to a safe depth
and will resurface again only
in later years;
Some brisk fall morning,
drinking coffee on her porch,
she will have a vision
of an ungiven gift
from a busy father.

The Way I Love You

The most difficult thing
is to love
without claim,
to trust
without owning,
to give up the
safety of preconception;

If we are lucky,
those whom we love
will never be
who we imagine
or want;
They will never do
as we expect;

The soul,
too virile
to be contained
by our simple expectations,
commands it's own
unique destiny;

We can never know
the people we love;
Their truth is far

more glorious
and alive
than we could
ever invent;

Rather,
we love by allowing
something uncontrollable
to unfold,
and those willing to
travel bravely
along that vibrant edge,
if only for the briefest moment,
can never love
any other way again.